HOW TO BE A
BiBLE
BRAINIAC

CF4•K

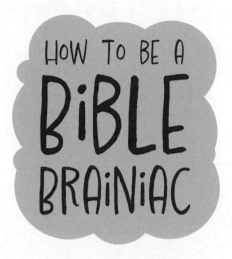

HOW TO BE A BiBLE BRAiNiAC

Knowing the One True God

CATHERINE MACKENZIE

CF4•K

10 9 8 7 6 5 4 3 2 1

Copyright © Christian Focus Publications 2023

ISBN: 978-1-5271-0975-9
Ebook: 978-1-5271-1113-4

Published by
Christian Focus Publications Ltd,
Geanies House, Fearn, Ross-shire,
IV20 1TW, Great Britain

www.christianfocus.com

Cover by Martyn Smith

Page Design and internal art by Pete Barnsley
(CreativeHoot.com)

Scripture quotations marked (NIV) are taken from the Holy Bible, New International Version®, NIV® Copyright ©1973, 1978, 1984, 2011 by Biblica, Inc.® Used by permission. All rights reserved worldwide.

Scripture quotations marked (ESV) are from The Holy Bible, English Standard Version, copyright © 2001 by Crossway Bibles, a publishing ministry of Good News Publishers. Used by permission. All rights reserved. ESV Text Edition: 2011.

Printed by Bell and Bain, Glasgow

This book is dedicated to three
new family members

William Sutherland Ross

Alan Macleod and

Samuel Williams

May you grow in the grace and knowledge of our
Lord and Saviour Jesus Christ *(2 Peter 3:18).*

CONTENTS

DON'T BUST YOUR BRAIN!

Don't lose your head.

To gain a minute.

You need your head.

Your brains are in it! *(Burma Shave Sign)*

I'm sure you know that your brain is very important. It gets you up in the morning.

It tells you when you need to eat your lunch.

It reminds you to turn right or left when you want to get somewhere.

Your brain stores all sorts of information inside – words and pictures, directions and instructions.

 EXTRA FACT: *Your brain weighs 1.3 kg and generates enough electricity to power a lightbulb.*

It's your brain that knows about your world, your family, your friends and God. Just as it's important to put information into your head so that you don't get hurt or lost – it's important to put the right information about God into your brain. Without the correct information you could find yourself believing a lie. It's only through finding out what the truth is that you will spot a fraud! And there are a lot of frauds out there. However, if you are to be a true Bible Brainiac you need to know God himself – not just facts about him. So, being a Bible Brainiac needs more than books. It's more than knowing facts. Reading good books is important – but to really know God you need more than just information.

Many people think they know God but in reality they don't. They believe a lie or a fiction. Many people know about God but they don't actually know him. More about that later. For now, keep your brain in gear because God made your brain and it's a serious piece of kit. Your brain is very cool. It's amazing. It's mind-boggling even.

Did you know that before you were born your brain was gathering information and learning what to do with it?

A baby inside the womb starts to hear at eighteen weeks. They can use their eyes at eight weeks old. But the human brain begins even earlier than that – at six weeks old. From that point on the human brain is working at sorting out all the information that comes its way – through touch, taste, smell, hearing and eyesight.

EXTRA FACT: *At the same time as the brain starts to function during Week 6 the unborn baby also starts to form taste-buds and begins to hiccup!*

Your brain does a lot even before you've chewed a book into a moist pulpy mess in your crib. A baby's brain has thought about and remembered all the different things its little baby eyes have looked at, and its little baby ears have listened to. The youngest baby has a brain that is faster and cleverer than a super-computer!

You may not be a scientist, or a librarian, you may not even have passed an exam – yet God has made you very smart.

Your brain judges the distance between your hand and the table and you're able to grab a cup and pour a drink. The calculations involved in that simple action are humongous.

How many times in your life have you brushed your teeth? Thousands probably. From the very first time you did it your brain has learned how much force it usually takes to brush your teeth and how hard you need to hold the brush in order not to drop it. However, your brain also does something else. Each time you brush your teeth your brain realises that there are other things that might happen to make you drop the brush. Your brain has learned over time that it doesn't know everything. So, every time you brush your teeth and grip hold of the brush your brain tells your hand to grip the brush a little bit tighter and firmer just in case.[1]

So, pat yourself on the back, you are a genius, at least at getting a cookie out of the jar and into your mouth without dropping it. God has created you as a true masterpiece – you're brilliant. There are so many things that he has made you able to do and learn to do. But you're more than just brain cells and information. There's more to you than skin, bones, neurons, and a funky hair style.

BIBLE PROOF

If any of you lacks wisdom, you should ask God, who gives generously to all without finding fault, and it will be given to you *(James 1:5 NIV)*.

- Do you know God?
- What is he like?
- Does he know you?

Ask Yourself

---

1 Get a grip: The neuroscience of how we pick things up, The Boston Globe – https://www.bostonglobe.com/ideas/2015/08/27/get-grip-the-neuroscience-how-pick-things/3XPqgZMVEgMPmlYX0cMooK/story.html

SKIN AND BONES!

You have a body but God has made you with a soul – that's the real you. And it's that real you that really needs to know him. There is more to knowledge than books, science, or mathematics. Facts are just one sort of knowledge. Wisdom is another.

God has made you in his image. What does that mean? Well you look at your own image whenever you look in a mirror. When you choose clothes or get a new hair cut you are thinking about your body image – the way you look. But there is more to image than that. When you are thinking of your image, the way you speak and behave also comes into play. You probably think about the way you look physically, and the way you appear to others more than you realise. When you want to fit into a group you might think about the way you sound and appear to those people. However, being made in God's image is more than your skin and bones. It means that God created human beings to be like him.

When an artist creates an image of someone in a painting or sculpture, they are making something for people to look at. The image in the gallery or town square is a representation of another person. The artist wants you to think about that person. Human beings were made in God's image so that they would show or reflect who God is. There is something in you, something about you, that should tell others something about God.

The next time you look in the mirror remember this – you are a mirror that shows the world what God is like. Even if you don't believe in God. When you create something artistic – it reflects the creative power of God who made the world in all its beauty. When you realise something is right or wrong, you are reflecting God. Someone who trusts God reflects him even more.

When you trust and love God, with all your heart, your life becomes a truer image of God, your Creator, and Jesus, your Saviour.

The thoughts you think. The emotions you feel. The words you say. The deeds you do. These all show the power, beauty and nature of God.

When we turn from our sin to trust in Jesus Christ the spoiled image is gradually restored.

One day that sin-spoiled image will be made perfect once again when God takes the believer to heaven through death. A hard thought to think about, but when you trust in God even death has hope.

There will come a day when even a believer's body will be made perfect. I wonder what that will be like? But let's get back to being a Bible Brainiac.

Another word for that is *wisdom*.

Wisdom is really important. Worldly wisdom happens when you know information and you know what to do with that information. It often comes with experience, which is why old people are usually called old and wise. An older person knows lots of things. They have real skills. They know how to do something and do it well. An old person will know something about someone – how old they are, where they live, and information like that. But they also know what that person needs and how to care for them. That's wisdom.

Godly wisdom is something even more important than that. It is a knowledge and understanding of God that helps us to make good decisions and follow God's directions in our lives. That sort of wisdom doesn't come with age, it doesn't come from being clever. It comes from truly knowing God and trusting in him. Wisdom is a gift from God. It's not something you earn or work for. It's a free gift from God to you.

That's magnificent. How amazing to be given such wonderful knowledge without any exams to pass! There aren't enough words to describe how brilliant God is.

True wisdom is realising that we are sinners, and that God requires sin-free perfection. But what is sin? What is a sinner?

You might not think you do anything wrong because you haven't ended up in jail or done anything that would get you in trouble with the police, your teacher or even your next-door neighbour! But the Bible says that all have sinned – so that means everyone has fallen short of God's perfect standard.

In a nut-shell that is what sin means – missing the mark. Not being perfect. Sin is whenever you do, say or think something that is against God's law. It is also when you don't do, say or think what he wants you to. Human beings sin by nature. But that's not an excuse. We're still responsible for everything we do and don't do. So we're sinners. God justly demands perfection and cannot stand to look on sin. It must be punished. So what can we do? Is there anything that we can do to sort things out? No. We cannot help ourselves.

Thankfully, God has not abandoned us. Although we deserve God's anger in his love and mercy he has made a rescue. God sent his one and only Son to this earth as a baby so that he would live the perfect sinless life instead of us. Jesus took God's anger by dying in our place. When we trust in Christ God's anger is dealt with, and sinners can come to God. Instead of being God's enemy forgiven sinners are his friends and even his beloved family.

Trusting in Jesus and what he has done is the key to unlocking true wisdom.

BIBLE PROOF

All have sinned *(Romans 3:23 ESV)*.

For the wages of sin is death, but the free gift of God is eternal life in Christ Jesus our Lord *(Romans 6:23 ESV)*.

- What would an image of you be like?

- How can you show the real God in your life?

BIBLE PROOF

You are my friends if you do what I command you *(John 15:14 ESV)*.

A man of many companions may come to ruin, but there is a friend who sticks closer than a brother *(Proverbs 18:24 ESV)*.

A baby recognises its mother at three months old. But a baby won't realise that the image in the mirror is them until they are about eighteen months old.

God said, "Let us make mankind in our image, in our likeness." *(Genesis 1:26 NIV).*

GETTING TO KNOW YOU!

Just as there are different kinds of knowledge, there are different ways to know someone.

Perhaps you know a lot of information about the President of the United States. You decide to enter a quiz and make him your special subject. You've read about him on the Internet and you've researched his family, his background and everything he has done. You know how tall he is, how much he weighs and you even know

what his favourite breakfast cereal is (at the moment it's Kelloggs Special K). You answer all the questions correctly, but if you've never met him do you really know him?

Perhaps you have met the President of the United States. Maybe you were standing in line and you waved at him as he walked through your town. You shook his hand and got a selfie. But he doesn't know your name – and you've never spent any time with him. You know he wants everyone to vote for him at the next election, but you're not what you would call *friends*. Even though you've met, you don't know each other.

However, perhaps you really do know the President of the United States. There will be some people who do – friends and family, people who work in his office. They don't need to read a book to find out about him. They don't need to join a queue to shake his hand. They know him in a very different way. They know about him. They know what he wants, but they also know who he is. His friends and family know his name and his family might even have a nick name for him that nobody else can use. It's only the president's children that can call him 'Daddy' or 'Pop' or 'Popsicle'.

There are three different kinds of knowing here – knowing facts about the President, knowing his face and then knowing him.

You might know facts about God, and when someone talks about him you might say, 'Oh that's God they're talking about,' but knowing God himself is more than that.

To know someone you need to spend time with them. So, do you get to know God by simply spending time with him?

You might go to church every week. Maybe you've got a Bible on your bookshelf. Perhaps you've even slotted God into your diary – that's fine. But do you have him in your heart? That means do you love him? If you are really going to know God and be a true Bible Brainiac you need to love him and trust in him. You need to love God with all your heart, soul and mind. Because, just as God created your amazing mind, he has made all of you. God made your mind and he has made your soul. Your soul is the real you, the part of you that chooses to love and obey God or not. God gave you a body to exist in and every part of you was created for one reason: to give honour and glory to God.

Spending time with God is important, but going to church and reading your Bible are not things that instantly make you know God. Church attendance and Bible reading are not steps one and two in the Get-to-know-God recipe. You can't say, 'I absolutely know God because I've been to eighty-seven church services and haven't missed Sunday school once.' Another thing you can't say is, 'I've read every chapter and verse in the Bible so I definitely know God now!' Going to church and reading the Bible are great, but you don't know God and become his child by completing tasks.

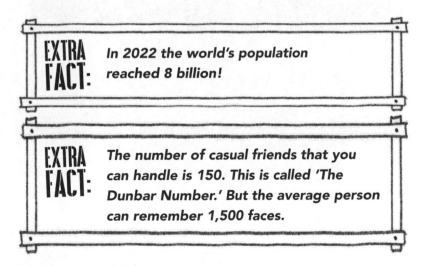

EXTRA FACT: *In 2022 the world's population reached 8 billion!*

EXTRA FACT: *The number of casual friends that you can handle is 150. This is called 'The Dunbar Number.' But the average person can remember 1,500 faces.*

Ask Yourself

- What is a true friend?
- Is God your friend?
- How many people do you know?
- If there was a quiz about you what questions would be asked?
- How do you get to know a new friend?
- How do you know if someone knows God?

IT ALL STARTS WITH GOD!

To really know God actually starts with God – it doesn't start with you. God knows you well. He is the one that takes you into his family. God opens your heart and makes a home there. He makes you love him. You give yourself to God because he has given himself to you. He changes you and instead of loving yourself first you begin to put God first. You turn away from sin to God. Another word for that is *repentance*.

When God shows you mercy, and brings you to repentance he changes your status from enemy of God to cherished child.

BIBLE PROOF

See what kind of love the Father has given to us, that we should be called children of God; and so we are *(1 John 3:1-2 ESV)*.

LÒÒK UP

Matthew 6:25-34; Hebrews 12:5-7.
How is God like a father here?

EXTRA FACT: **A family is a group of two or more people who live together and are related by birth, marriage, or adoption. There are 83.7 million families in the United States and 19.3 million families in the United Kingdom.**

How does God make you his child? Have you seen how a magnet attracts metal? If you put the magnet over the metal filings they come closer to the magnet and stick to it. God's power brings you close to him. He changes you so that you are attracted to him instead of sin. You want to please him instead of just pleasing yourself. That is the beginning of you knowing God. Really knowing God means that your heart, soul and mind love him. You think about him, and long to worship him and praise him. You belong to him. You are his child.

He is your Heavenly Father. When you look at God and see how good he is, you will realise – wow – that's what a truly good father is. He's perfect in all the best ways.

You will still not know everything there is to know about God. But when God changes your heart you will see that he really loves you and that you really need him. You will long to know him better so you will want to study his Word, to know the truth about him and what he wants. You will want to learn about God's identity. That is the start of a truly wonderful adventure.

A change will happen to you maybe suddenly or over a long period of time. But when God changes you, one day you will notice that reading the Bible is more precious to you. Sometimes when you listen to a talk about God, maybe in church or at a Bible study you will enjoy it even more than your favourite meal or junk food treat. When God saves you the Good News about Jesus Christ becomes delicious.

Fill yourself up with God and his Word like you do a tasty meal when your tummy is really rumbling! God gives you a satisfaction like nothing else!

The adventure of knowing God starts with becoming his friend. From then on the information that you get from reading God's Word, and listening to it being preached, make that friendship really shine!

Knowing God means that you agree to follow him for the rest of your life. But remember when you are trying to know more about God – God knows everything there is to know

EXTRA FACT: *Those who follow God and trust in his Son are given a special name and that's 'Disciple'.*

about you. He knows you very well. He knows you better than you know yourself!

What does God know about you? Well, he designed you – so he knows every building block that makes up your body. He knows your name, where you live, and how many hairs are on your head.

BIBLE PROOF I have called you by name, you are mine *(Isaiah 43:1 ESV)*.

And the Lord said to him, "Rise and go to the street called Straight, and at the house of Judas look for a man of Tarsus named Saul, for behold, he is praying" *(Acts 9:11 ESV)*.

But even the hairs of your head are all numbered *(Matthew 10:30 ESV)*.

God knows the things you like and dislike, he knows if you are shy or boisterous, he knows the things you do well and those things that you struggle with. He knows what you will do before you even know you're going to do it. He knows when you sit down and when you stand up. He knows all your thoughts. Even before a word has made it from your brain to your tongue, God knows what you are going to say!

From the very beginning God was involved in the intricate work of knitting you together inside the body of your mother. You are a true masterpiece. God knew you while you were in your mother's womb, and he knows the day that you will die.

BIBLE PROOF You know when I sit down and when I rise up; you discern my thoughts from afar *(Psalm 139:2 ESV)*.

Before a word is on my tongue, you LORD, know it completely *(Psalm 139:4 NIV)*.

You knitted me together in my mother's womb *(Psalm 139:13)*.

Your eyes saw my unformed body; all the days ordained for me were written in your book before one of them came to be *(Psalm 139:16 NIV)*.

God knows your soul. He knows whether your heart really loves him or not.

There isn't anything that you can hide from God. He knows it all.

God knows you and will never forget you. Do you know what it's like to be forgetful? I do. I have notes everywhere reminding me to do this or that. I have alarms that buzz on my phone to remind me that it's time to go somewhere. If I don't have a phone or a notebook around, but I still have a pen, I sometimes write the memo on my hand.

In the Bible there is a verse that teaches us that God never forgets about us and it's, Isaiah 49:16 'I have engraved you on the palms of my hands.' God isn't forgetful like we are – but this verse is just showing us that no matter what, God's mind is always on us. We are close to his heart.

BIBLE PROOF

Man looks at the outward appearance, but the Lord looks at the heart *(1 Samuel 16:7)*.

Nothing in all creation is hidden from God's sight *(Hebrews 4:13)*.

For the eyes of the Lord are on the righteous, and his ears are open to their prayer *(1 Peter 3:12)*.

Ask Yourself

- What makes a family?
- What does God do for his children?
- What are you really like?
- What seven words describe you? (Don't use colours or numbers.)
- Can you think of seven words to describe God?
- If you could choose a super-power what would it be? An invisibility cloak? A photographic memory?

GOD'S SUPERPOWERS!

God has a whole host of superpowers. In fact he is more than super powerful; he is all powerful.

One of God's super powers is a super gift he gives to sinners – the gift of salvation. Salvation is how he rescues sinners from the punishment their sin deserves. This can be done by God because he is all powerful, all knowing, and merciful.

No one is as powerful as God. Another word for that is *Omnipotent*.

You can't hide anything from God, and God knows everything about you because of another superpower unique to him – he is Omniscient – all knowing. This is part of his nature. It's not a gimmick. It's not something he acquired. It's his essence and identity.

God knows you as you really are. That is good – really it is! He loves you as you are. He doesn't love your sin – but he loves you even though you are a sinner. He already knows the worst about you. There are no dark secrets for him to discover – he knows them all.

There isn't anything that God doesn't know. We can't say that about ourselves. We're not all knowing. We never will be. In fact some of us struggle with remembering telephone numbers and birthdays. But thankfully knowing God isn't about being clever or even having a good memory. God has arranged it so that we can know him and know him well. Even though we will never know everything about God we can know everything that we need to know about ourselves and about God – right here and right now. The Bible teaches us all we need to know.

Everything about God is wonderful, marvellous and perfect. But there is one of his attributes or superpowers that is truly amazing. It's a very important part of his nature. The Bible tells us that God is love.

How does God show his love? He loves his Son. God has always been loving. God the Father, God the Son and God the Holy Spirit have always been in a relationship with each other and that relationship is loving.

God loves sinners. He loved the world so much that he sent his one and only Son. Look up the Bible verse John 3:16. God loves his people. God's Word tells us in Romans 8:38 that his love is so great that there is nothing that can separate those who trust in God from his loving heart.

By giving his Son, God has shown us how much he loves us. We receive his love as a free gift. We show how loving God is by giving that love to others.

How do you know that God's love is great? He loves sinners who do not deserve to be loved. He loves sinners so much that he was willing to pay a great price. God gave the life of his one and only Son. And God's love is great because he is generous with his love and doesn't hold back.

BIBLE PROOF At just the right time, when we were still powerless, Christ died for the ungodly. Very rarely will anyone die for a righteous person, though for a good person someone might possibly dare to die. But God demonstrates his own love for us in this: While we were still sinners, Christ died for us *(Romans 5:6-8 NIV)*.

LOOK UP

John 15:13

God's love is the greatest because it gives the greatest benefit – eternal life.

BIBLE PROOF For God so loved the world, that he gave his one and only Son, that whoever believes in him shall not perish but have eternal life *(John 3:16 NIV)*.

The Lord is compassionate and gracious, slow to anger, abounding in love *(Psalm 103:8 NIV)*.

Because of the Lord's great love we are not consumed, for his compassions never fail. They are new every morning; great is your faithfulness *(Lamentations 3: 22-23 NIV)*.

LÓÓK UP

Zephaniah 3:17 What does this verse tell us about God's love? At what events would you show your joy with loud singing?

LOOK UP Romans 5:8; 1 John 4:19; 1 John 4:9-11; Colossians 3:12-14; Ephesians 4:32; Jeremiah 31:3; Psalm 63:3. What do these verses tell us about God and about what humans need?

Ask Yourself

• How would you feel if everyone could read your thoughts?

• Why is it good that God knows all about you?

EXTRA FACT: Ten of the strongest animals in the world: Elephant; Eagle; Tiger; Goliath Grouper; Dung Beetle; Saltwater Crocodile; Anaconda; Blue Whale; Gorilla; Leafcutter Ant.

Here are some important things to know about you and God:

1. We are made by God – male or female.

2. We have a body that will die and a soul that will live forever.

3. We are sinners. We choose to disobey God instead of love him.

4. God is holy and hates sin.

5. He rules everything.

6. God can save us from sin.

7. He does this through his Son Jesus Christ who took the punishment for our sin by dying on the cross.

8. When we trust in Jesus Christ though we are sinners we can trust in the fact that God has saved us. He rescues sinners from the guilt and power of sin.

9. God has spoken to humanity through the Bible his Word and he has given us the Bible so that he can bring us to a saving knowledge of himself.

10. Knowing God means that we must respond to God by trusting in him and obeying him. We worship him for who he is.

All these amazing truths are there for us to discover. But how do we find out all these things?

GOD SAYS IT!

God tells us about himself in two ways. First, he uses nature but more important than that God has given us his Word. Nature shows us some things about ourselves, our world and that there must be a creator. God's Word gives us the real important information about him and how much we need God's forgiveness.

NATURE

Hundreds of years ago human beings didn't know as much about the earth as they do now. However, a human being would still have looked at the amazing animals, plants, sky, stars, and been astonished at how well everything fitted together. The sun shone every day in the sky giving warmth and light. The rain watered the ground making the plants grow. The animals and humans got all that they needed to live and breathe. Everything that happened on a daily basis was proof that there was an all-powerful Creator God. They could tell that God existed through what they could see and hear and experience in the world around them. When things went wrong with natural disasters, like floods and hurricanes, human beings would have realised that something wasn't right. They could see the good of creation and also the pain and hurt that took place when creation went wrong. Those two things should make anyone stop and ask, 'Who made this world? And why has it all gone wrong?'

BIBLE PROOF

When I look at your heavens, the work of your fingers, the moon and the stars, which you have set in place, what is man that you are mindful of him, and the son of man that you care for him? (Psalm 8:3,4 ESV).

The heavens declare the glory of God; the skies proclaim the work of his hands. Day after day they pour forth speech; night after night they display knowledge (Psalm 19:1-2 NIV).

Also look up Romans 1:19,20.

Nowadays, we know quite a bit more about our world than in the past. For example, did you know that the earth is just the right size – not too big and not too small. If the earth's crust was just ten feet thicker than it is or the oceans a few feet deeper, life on this planet would not be able to exist.

> **EXTRA FACT:** *The moon is about 239,000 miles away from the earth. The moon controls the movement of the oceans and if it was not as far away as it is, many cities would be submerged by tidal floods.*

Ask Yourself

• What do you love about nature and how does sin spoil it?

• What will it be like when God makes the new heavens and earth?

Our world has just the right amount of oxygen for us to be able to breathe. The atmosphere of earth protects us from the sun's radiation. There are so many things in the world that all fit together perfectly. If you were to write them all down and work them all out, you would have to admit that somehow, somewhere there must be a designer – one God who has created everything. Even when things go wrong in our world we realise that things are wrong because we've seen how they go right. When we see our wonderful world we should stop and wonder who made it? And when we see things going wrong we should stop and ask why? It wasn't designed to go wrong. Something must have happened. But what?

GOD'S WORD

When we ask what went wrong, that's when we should read God's Word: the Bible. Nature shouts out to us that there is a creator of the universe, but to find out what went wrong we need to read God's Word. You need to be a Bible Brainiac! Reading God's Word for yourself is very important. This is the way that God has chosen to introduce himself to you. The Bible is how you know what God actually said. Throughout history people have tried to take away from or add to God's Word – and that is very, very wrong.

BIBLE PROOF You shall not add to the word that I command you, nor take from it, that you may keep the commandments of the LORD your God that I command you *(Deuteronomy 4:2 ESV)*.

When you read God's Word, a good place to start is at the beginning in the book of Genesis. We read there a summary of how God created the world in six days. And we also find out about what went wrong.

When God made the earth, all the plants and animals and mankind, God was very pleased.

It was all good. It was designed perfectly. It worked very well and looked beautiful. The first man and woman, Adam and Eve, were made with something called free will. God didn't make puppets. He didn't make robots. He made living, breathing, decision-making men and women to love and worship him. But Adam and Eve chose to disobey him and that is when the order and perfection of creation broke.

We live in a world spoiled by sin. There is death, disease, murder, cheating, earthquakes, floods. Natural and man-made disasters. This destruction is something that we are responsible for because humanity chose and always has chosen sin rather than God.

You might be one of those people who think that it's not fair that we have to suffer for the sin of Adam and Eve. But the truth is that you and I are no different to Adam and Eve. In the same situation we would have made the same decision. We can't whine about things not being fair when God is completely fair and always just. Can you think of any day in your whole life when you didn't choose to sin? Has there been any time when you didn't have inside you a selfish thought, or a desire to have your own way? Have you always loved God with a perfect love? The answer is no. Things went wrong in the Garden of Eden but things go wrong in our hearts and minds every day we live.

Thankfully, the Bible is not a book that just tells us about how things went wrong. It tells us about how God made things right again.

In the first few chapters of Genesis God made a promise that he would rescue his people from the power and punishment of sin. God had a rescue plan. Did he suddenly come up with this idea when he realised that Adam and Eve had messed things up? Was he caught off-guard? No. God had planned this rescue mission from before the beginning of time. Before Adam and Eve sinned he knew what they were going to do – and he knew what he had to do to save sinners from the guilt and punishment of their sin.

God promised to send a Saviour to the world who would destroy the power of sin. That Saviour was God's very own Son who would willingly be born as a human to live a perfect life and then take the punishment for sin. To prove that sin and death had been defeated God's Son would then come back to life again. This is called the Resurrection.

A lot of the Bible from Genesis onwards is about how sin spoils everything and how God punishes sin. Another word for that is *justice*. But then throughout the Bible we also read of how God forgives sinners, cleansing them from its guilt and delivering them from its power. Another word for that is *grace* or *mercy*.

Justice is when someone is treated in the way that they deserve.

Grace is the character of God when he shows us his undeserved mercy.

Mercy is when someone who deserves to be punished is not punished and set free.

That has been God's rescue plan from before time began. That is salvation.

The Good News of Jesus Christ. AKA – the gospel!

BIBLE PROOF

God saw everything that he had made, and behold, it was very good *(Genesis 1:31 ESV).*

The law of the LORD is perfect, reviving the soul; the testimony of the LORD is sure, making wise the simple; the precepts of the LORD are right, rejoicing the heart *(Psalm 19:7-8 ESV).*

All Scripture is breathed out by God and profitable for teaching, for reproof, for correction, and for training in righteousness *(2 Timothy 3:16 ESV).*

Here are some important things to know about God's Word:

1. God has given us the Bible.

   For no prophecy was ever produced by the will of man, but men spoke from God as they were carried along by the Holy Spirit (2 Peter 1:21 ESV).

2. God gives us the ability to understand the Bible.

   Then He opened their minds to understand the Scriptures (Luke 24:45 ESV).

3. God's Word is important to life.

   But he answered, "It is written, "'Man shall not live by bread alone, but by every word that comes from the mouth of God.'" (Matthew 4:4 ESV).

4. God's Word is true.

   Every word of God proves true;
   he is a shield to those who take
   refuge in him (Proverbs 30:5 ESV).

5. God's Word is our guide.

   Your word is a lamp to my feet and
   a light to my path (Psalm 119:105 ESV).

6. It is the Word of God that brings
   you to faith in God.

   So faith comes from hearing, and
   hearing through the word of Christ
   (Romans 10:17 ESV).

GOD NEVER CHANGES!

One of the amazing things about God is that he never changes. That's wonderful.  When we know what he is like we can trust him to be like that for ever. He is always going to be fair and when you trust in his love you know that his love will always be there – because he never changes. He's not a here-today-gone-tomorrow sort of friend.

We can't say that about ourselves. Do you have a height chart in your kitchen where over the years a parent has marked on the wall how tall you are? Year by year that mark climbs up the wall marking off how much you have grown since the previous year.

That's just one small way that you change. You change in other ways too. Your face will look different, your hair too. You might have loved dinosaurs as a little kid, but now you prefer football. Maybe you used to love blackcurrant squash, but now you drink coffee. Cappuccino anyone? Your tastes have changed.

But God never changes. Someone who is very old will have changed a lot over their lifetime, but that doesn't apply to God. He is perfect – holy – he does not need to change. In fact, if he was to change he would not improve because he is the best he could ever be.

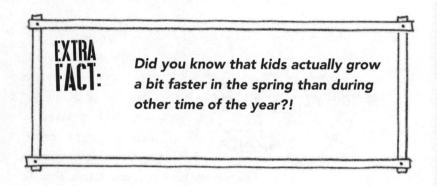

EXTRA FACT: *Did you know that kids actually grow a bit faster in the spring than during other time of the year?!*

One of the other amazing things about God is that he is a planner and an organiser – as always the best planner and organiser. He planned out salvation before the world was made and he did everything required to bring that plan of salvation to success.

God's Word was written so that people could hear the promises of salvation and then recognise the real Saviour when he came.

Jesus fulfils so many of the promises that God made in the Old Testament.

Most of the Bible was written hundreds of years before Jesus' birth. Yet, it clearly points out that Jesus would be a descendant of Jacob, and of David, and that he would be born in Bethlehem and that his mother would be a virgin. Even the arrival of the wise men was foretold.

"I the LORD; do not change" (*Malachi 3:6 ESV*).

Also look up: *James 1:17.*

A star will come out of Jacob; a scepter will rise out of Israel *(Numbers 24:17 NIV).*

But you Bethlehem Ephrathah, though you are small among the clans of Judah, out of you will come for me one who will be ruler over Israel *(Micah 5:2 NIV).*

The virgin will conceive and give birth to a son, and will call him Immanuel *(Isaiah 7:14 NIV).*

May the kings of Sheba and Seba present him gifts *(Psalm 72:10 NIV).*

It's amazing to read about the birth and life of Jesus, his words, his miracles, his death and resurrection and to realise that this was all part of God's plan. Before the world was made God the Father, God the Son and God the Holy Spirit planned for creation and salvation. God's plan was that sinners would be able to know God in a very special way, through Jesus Christ.

When we read these prophecies in the Old Testament and then later read in the New Testament how Jesus fulfils them, this gives us a confidence in the Word of God and in God himself. What God said would happen has happened so we can trust that this will always be the case.

God has promised that Jesus will return, that God's people will have eternal life, that there will one day be a new creation without sin or fear or heartache.

We don't know when any of that will happen – but God does. He knows everything that there is to know about everything. The word for that is *Omniscient*.

He is all powerful or *Omnipotent*. There is nothing and no one who is stronger than him. He is everywhere at all times. Another word for that is *Omni-present*.

He is certainly different to us in some very important ways. He is one and he is three! What? Does that puzzle you? I told you that God is different. Well, this is one way that he is. There is just one God but this includes three persons. Another word for this is *Godhead*: God the Father, God the Son and God the Holy Spirit. Sometimes you might hear people using the word *Trinity* – but it's not a word you will find in the Bible. That is a word that Christians came up with in order to describe an important piece of information about God. This is difficult to comprehend. But God is very different from us. Some things we can understand about God. Some things we just have to marvel at!

God the Father, God the Son and God the Holy Spirit are the same. They are one God but three persons: equally powerful and glorious. They were all together at creation and they act together in the work of saving sinners. Salvation was God the Father's plan, Jesus made it happen and the Holy Spirit makes that salvation work in you by showing you that you need it and guiding you to accept salvation as a free gift.

Another way God is different is that he is a spirit. When you describe yourself you use words like tall or short, curly or freckled. Because he is a spirit you can't use words like these to describe God. The Bible describes God as having arms and hands and eyes and ears – but that's just to help us understand his power and what he can do. Only Jesus Christ the Son, who put on humanity, has a body.

There is not a real picture of God. In fact the Bible says that it is wrong to create an image of God. We don't have a photo of God the Father or of Jesus either – and there is

BIBLE PROOF Surely the arm of the Lord is not too short to save, nor his ear too dull to hear *(Isaiah 59:1 NIV)*.

not even a physical description of Jesus. That is because really knowing God means knowing his character – not a face. Really knowing Jesus is the same. It's more important to know the way Jesus behaved and loved, rather than what style of hair he had or how tall he was.

If someone draws a picture of Jesus they will often imagine what he would have looked like. But are these pictures accurate?

The Bible gives us a hint in the Book of Isaiah. There we are told in a prophecy that Jesus would not look like a majestic important person, he wouldn't even look that handsome.

BIBLE PROOF

He had no beauty or majesty to attract us to him, nothing in his appearance that we should desire him *(Isaiah 53:2 NIV)*.

Sometimes when people imagine what Jesus would have looked like they assume he would have been good looking – but history has changed what we think about good looks. The good looks of one hundred years ago look weird to us today. So, it's not a good idea to draw an image of God or Jesus. We will get it wrong and God doesn't want us to do it. So it's not wise.

Knowing what Jesus looked like is not important. Just because you haven't met Jesus in the flesh doesn't mean that you can't know him. Jesus said, 'Blessed are those who have not seen and yet have believed.' (John 20:29). One day those who trust in Jesus will see him face to face and that will be wonderful. They will be filled with an inexpressible joy. Read 1 Peter 1:8. For now we know his character and that's the most important thing.

LOÒK UP

Isaiah 53 and Psalm 22. Now look up the following verses in the New Testament and see how they match: *Luke 23:21-23; Matthew 27:12-14; 27:27-31; 27:35; 27:39; 27:43; 27:46; Luke 23:32; John 19:37, 20:27; John 19:28; Luke 23:34; John 19:23; 2 Corinthians 5:21.*

- Can you describe yourself with verbs and not nouns?
- What verbs describe God?

Ask Yourself

WHAT NEXT?

To know God we need to know the things that happened in Jesus' life. How did God the Son become a human being? How did God make that happen? Well, it happened in a similar way to how you came into the world, but also it was very different.

Jesus Christ the Son of God took on a body when he was conceived in the womb of his mother Mary. This is also called the Incarnation. Jesus' conception was different but his birth was like ours. His mother did not have sex or physical relations with another man. She was a virgin. It was the power of the Holy Spirit who overshadowed her and brought life into her womb. Mary and Joseph, Jesus' mother and earthly father, were both told by God that their son, Jesus, would save his people from their sins. He would be the Son of the Most High God. Jesus is God and Man in the same person.

BIBLE PROOF Behold, the virgin shall conceive and bear a son, and shall call his name Immanuel (*Isaiah 7:14*).

When his mother Mary had been betrothed to Joseph, before they came together she was found to be with child from the Holy Spirit (*Matthew 1:18 ESV*).

EXTRA FACT: *694, 685 children were born in the U.K. in 2021. In the USA the number was 3.66 million.*

Not only was Jesus' birth different. Jesus' life was different too. He was without sin. He lived and walked and ate and slept like us yet his life was one that showed what a perfect human being should be.

Sin had scarred the perfect human nature God designed in Adam and Eve. But Jesus lived that perfect human life because we cannot.

His death was different too. (This is often called the Crucifixion because he died by being nailed to a wooden cross.) Although Jesus was killed by his enemies, he actually died because it was God the Father's plan. Jesus died so that sinners could be set free from sin – set free from the guilt and the punishment they deserved.

After his death his body was brought back to life and this is called the Resurrection. Jesus' death was only temporary. He was in the grave for three days before he was brought back to life. God's plan worked. Death was defeated. Sin was crushed. God won the battle against evil.

After that Jesus returned to heaven. This is called the Ascension. One day Jesus will return again. The first time he came to earth as a baby, the second time he will be exalted above all creation - the victorious King of kings.

BIBLE PROOF For we do not have a high priest who is unable to sympathize with our weaknesses, but one who in every respect has been tempted as we are, yet without sin *(Hebrews 4:15 ESV).*

Another thing that is different about Jesus' death is that although he was physically attacked by his enemies, in the end it wasn't their actions that killed him – it was his decision. How do we know that? We read in Matthew 27:50 that Jesus 'gave up his spirit'.

So, though others committed the act of murder it was God's plan that Jesus died and it was Jesus' choice when his spirit left his body.

We also read that when the soldiers came around to check on Jesus, they were surprised to see he was already dead. Further evidence that Jesus' death was different and that God was in control!

BIBLE PROOF

And when Jesus had cried out again in a loud voice, he gave up his spirit *(Matthew 27:50 NIV)*.

Death is swallowed up in victory. O death, where is your victory? O death, where is your sting? *(1 Corinthians 15: 54-55 ESV)*.

Something else makes his death different ... he didn't stay dead. That doesn't normally happen!

BIBLE PROOF

But on the first day of the week, at early dawn, they went to the tomb, taking the spices they had prepared. And they found the stone rolled away from the tomb, but when they went in they did not find the body of the Lord Jesus *(Luke 24:1-3 ESV)*.

And that's not the end. The physically resurrected Jesus returned to heaven. In between his resurrection and ascension many eye witnesses saw him alive and gave evidence to that fact.

While he blessed them, he parted from them and was carried up into heaven *(Luke 24:51 ESV)*.

After that the disciples returned to Jerusalem with great joy, worshipping God at the temple.

They were not left on their own as God sent the third person of the Godhead, the Holy Spirit, to be their helper.

And that's not the end of the story either!

When the day of Pentecost arrived and the Holy Spirit came, the church grew. The disciples who had been scared fishermen became brave preachers of God's Word.

As a result the gospel spread around the globe and it is still spreading.

If you trust in Jesus you are now part of that story and when you give the glory to God you are like the disciples – you are being used by God to spread the Good News! Just as God gave the scared fishermen courage he will do the same for you!

EXTRA FACT: *Three weird facts about the natural world: Most people can't lick their own elbow; pigs cannot look up into the sky; everyone's tongue print is different.*

WHAT GOD IS REALLY LIKE

Have you or anyone in your family ever applied for a new job? When that happens a person needs to send in an application and something called a C.V. or resume. This tells the interviewers what the interviewee is like and what things they are good at doing.

They write some basic information such as their name, age, address and qualifications. But then they add a little sparkle to the whole thing and try to show through words why they are the perfect choice for the job that they are applying for.

God doesn't need a C.V., or resume but if you were to write a job description for God in order to explain to people what he is really like and why he is the BEST, it might look something like this:

Name:

God the Father, God the Son, God the Holy Spirit

Address:

Our God is in the heavens; he does all that he pleases *(Psalm 115: 3 ESV)*.

Personal Information:

God is a Spirit: Being then God's offspring, we ought not to think that the divine being is like gold or silver or stone, an image formed by the art and imagination of man *(Acts 17:29 ESV)*.

God is Infinite or limitless: Great is the LORD, and greatly to be praised, and his greatness is unsearchable *(Psalm 145:3 ESV)*.

God is Eternal, existing forever: Before the mountains were brought forth, or ever you had formed the earth and the world, from everlasting to everlasting you are God *(Psalm 90:2 ESV)*.

But you, O LORD, are enthroned forever; you are remembered throughout all generations *(Psalm 102:12 ESV)*.

God is Unchangeable: Jesus Christ is the same yesterday and today and forever *(Hebrews 13:8 ESV)*.

God has Wisdom: Oh, the depth of the riches and wisdom and knowledge of God! *(Romans 11:33 NIV).*

He has power: The Lord is the everlasting God, the Creator of the ends of the earth. He does not faint or grow weary; his understanding is unsearchable (*Isaiah 40:28 ESV).*

He is holy, perfect and glorious: God is Light, and in Him there is no darkness at all (*1 John 1:5 ESV)*

He is just: He has fixed a day in which He will judge the world in righteousness. (*Acts 17:31)*

For I the Lord love justice; I hate robbery and wrong (*Isaiah 61:8).*

He is good: The Lord, the Lord God, merciful and gracious, long-suffering, and abounding in goodness and truth (*Exodus 34:6).*

He is true: Every word of God proves true (*Proverbs 30:5).*

He is love: We know how much God loves us, and we have put our trust in his love. God is love, and all who live in love live in God, and God lives in them (*1 John 4:16).*

All these characteristics of God are also called Attributes. They are who and what God is. It's not that a bit of God is true and another bit is loving and another bit just. Everything about God is all of these things. One attribute isn't added to the other – everything about God is true, just, and good. He has always been all of these things.

You and I are given everything from God – all life is from him. But God's life is in him already. He doesn't receive life from anything or anyone else. As a human being you need certain things to survive, like air and water. Everything that was made needs something else to exist. But God does not need anything else to exist or live.

God didn't make the world because he needed to. He didn't make men and women because he needed people to worship him or be friends with him. God doesn't need anything. Human beings make houses to shelter in, boats to travel in. We plant crops so that we can eat them and fuel our lives. God has no need of anything like that.

BIBLE PROOF The God who made the world and everything in it, being Lord of heaven and earth, does not live in temples made by man, nor is he served by human hands, as though he needed anything, since he himself gives to all mankind life and breath and everything (Acts 17:24-25 ESV).

If you believe in God your belief in him doesn't make God any better or more important than he already is. If you don't believe in God it doesn't make him less important either.

And although God wants us to worship him, obey him, and to live our lives in a way that honours him, he doesn't actually need our help. We can serve him but he doesn't need servants. He wants us to serve – but if we don't it doesn't make him less than he is. The God who doesn't need anyone to help him has, however, chosen to use his obedient human children in the work that he wants completed.

A river gets bigger as the rain falls and it makes its way towards the sea. But God doesn't get bigger than he is. He is immeasurable. He is everything that he needs to be. He needs nothing else to make him better as he is the best and the most perfect, exactly as he is.

He doesn't need you – but you need him. And he wants sinners to find their satisfaction in him.

Sometimes we think we can find our fulfilment in the love of another person: a boyfriend or girlfriend. Maybe you think you might find fulfilment in a career, or in accomplishments such as art or music. When all these things are done in order to glorify God then they can be fulfilling. But our ultimate fulfilment as human beings will always be in God himself.

The chief purpose of humanity is to glorify God and to enjoy him forever. You don't need to be a brilliant, intelligent, exciting, cool, fashionable person to be on

God's team. God needs no one, but he will work through anyone who trusts in him. And trust is simple enough for a child to do – sometimes children find trusting easier to do than adults.

Trusting in God is not something he needs you to do, it's something YOU need to do. There are other things you should do but the most important thing is to realise that Jesus has done everything necessary to save you from your sins. After that, all you have to do is ask God for forgiveness, thank him for all he has done and live for Jesus because he died for you.

BIBLE PROOF Trust in the Lord with all your heart, and do not lean on your own understanding. In all your ways acknowledge him, and he will make straight your paths *(Proverbs 3:5-6 ESV)*.

EXTRA FACT: *Studying God is also called Theology. Theos is a Greek word for God. The word Ology means a subject of study.*

Ask Yourself

- What are the most important things someone needs to know about God?

- Where do you find out about the one true God?

- What is the main purpose of a human being? (1 Corinthians 6:20; 1 Corinthians 10:31)

- What are the two main things that the Bible teaches us? (John 5:39; John 20:31; Deuteronomy 10:12-13.)

Here are some important things to know about God's world:

1. God made the world.

    The LORD is the everlasting God, the Creator of the ends of the earth (Isaiah 40:28 ESV).

    The earth is the LORD's and everything in it, the world, and all who live in it (Psalm 24:1 NIV).

2. This world is not eternal and it will end. God will make a new world.

    The World and its desires pass away, but whoever does the will of God lives forever (1 John 2:17 NIV).

    I will create new heavens and a new earth (Isaiah 65:17 NIV).

    Then I saw a new heaven and a new earth for the first heaven and the first earth had passed away and there was no longer any sea (Revelation 21:1 NIV).

3. You will not be in this world forever, not even for that long.

For we brought nothing into the world and we can take nothing out of it (1 Timothy 6:7 NIV).

Mortals, born of woman, are of few days and full of trouble. They spring up like flowers and wither away; like fleeting shadows, they do not endure (Job 14:1-2 NIV).

5. This world has been spoiled by sin. The world is against God.

Don't you know that friendship with the world means enmity against God? Therefore, anyone who chooses to be a friend of the world becomes an enemy of God (James 4:4 NIV).

6. Your soul is more valuable than the world and all it offers.

What good will it be for someone to gain the whole world, yet forfeit their soul? Or what can anyone give in exchange for their soul? (Matthew 16:26 NIV).

COPYING CHRIST!

When you get up in the morning what image do you see first? Do you go and look at your brother's face first of all or the dog's? It's more likely that you go to the mirror to check your own image. You check that everything is in order – all nice and tidy, well presented.

We can check that things are right with our souls by making sure they match up to God's image. And one way of doing that is by reading God's Word and copying Jesus.

When you look at your thoughts and actions do you think 'I'm like God.' Probably not. Because in the Garden of Eden sin spoiled creation and your humanity is part of that creation that was spoiled.

However, occasionally when you look at human beings you see their wonderful potential – there is still something there that hints at the fact that God made us to be better than we are. God certainly wants those who trust in him to become the people he meant them to be. He wants us to be like Jesus.

BIBLE PROOF

So God created mankind in his own image, in the image of God he created them; male and female he created them *(Genesis 1:27 NIV)*.

If you are a follower of Jesus, God is working on you every day - renewing you - making you even more of a master piece than you already are! There is a special word for this – *sanctification*. You are being made more like Jesus.

BIBLE PROOF

Do not lie to one another, seeing that you have put off the old self with its practices and have put on the new self, which is being renewed in knowledge after the image of its creator *(Colossians 3:9-10)*.

EXTRA FACT: **Until the late 17th century, the word 'family' included not only your relatives but also any servants in the household.**

Family resemblances are funny. Imagine that you are standing in a train station when you spot someone waiting for the same train as you. You feel as though you have seen this man before, but you know you haven't. You look at the guy a bit closer and realise that he has the same curly ginger hair as Bob, a friend of yours that you met at camp last summer. Strangely enough he is tossing some change from one hand to the other in exactly the same way as Bob does. He's even whistling a tune and Bob was always doing that. Might it be possible that this stranger is actually related to Bob? Now imagine that you pluck up the courage and go over to this guy and ask him, 'Are you related to Bob?' and then this guy turns to you and says, 'Do you mean Robert Black? Sure, I know him, he's my younger brother!'

Well, that would be amazing. But that is the way families are sometimes – we resemble one another. Even when we aren't related biologically we grow to be like the people we love and live with. When God takes you into his family he is adopting you. A child who is adopted into a family is just as much a part of that family as a child who has been born into it. God adopts us into his family so that you and I are now younger siblings of Jesus Christ, God's Son. God is now our Heavenly Father.

If you have trusted in Jesus to save you from your sin you are now part of God's family, so Jesus is your older brother. He is the Son of God. God is his Father. Eventually, with the Holy Spirit's help, you will become more like Jesus Christ – and people who see you will recognise a family resemblance.

It won't be hair, or eyes or any facial features but instead it will be the characteristics of Jesus. God wants us to imitate him. In much the same way a little child likes to imitate what his parents or older siblings do.

So what does it mean to be a child of God? The family you live with is unique to you. Do people look at the things you and your siblings do and say, 'That's so typical of them!' My brother-in-law loves to set off fireworks and so do his brothers and his kids. It seems to be a family thing!

LOOK UP

Ephesians 5:1-2; Romans 8:29; Ephesians 1:5; Galatians 4:6-7; 2 Corinthians 6:18.

What does each verse tell you about being part of God's family?

Some families have traits and characteristics. The following are character traits that you should display in your life if you are adopted into God's family. They glorify God and show the world what God your Father is really like.

You should demonstrate:

LOVE

Love is a word we often use when we talk about romance or friendship. But there is more to love than that. In fact, in the Bible there is a special word to describe the love of God. This word is a Greek word *Agape*. It describes God's great sacrificial love for human beings but it also describes the love a human being has for God. This is a spiritual love and it is created by God. We are able to love him because he first loved us. This love is much greater than the natural love we have for friends and family. 'It flows from a heart that has been changed by God the Holy Spirit.'[2]

JOY

Joy is more than being happy. You can be happy about a football score or your new shoes. Joy is deeper than that. It is better because it comes from God and lasts even when we are feeling sad and troubled. Joy is both thrilling and peaceful at the same time! And the joy a Christian has is because God loves them and has saved them through Jesus Christ. God's children receive it through the Holy Spirit when he opens their hearts to the beauty of Jesus. Joy is that feeling you get when you read God's Word and your heart leaps because it knows you are meeting with Jesus. Sometimes you will feel like that when you are singing praises to God or when you are spending time with other people who love and trust in Jesus.

---

2 *The Fruit of the Spirit* by R.C. Sproul https://www.monergism.com/fruit-spirit-r-c-sproul#:~:text=It%20was%20ratified,a%20judgmental%20spirit.

BIBLE PROOF

The kingdom of God is not a matter of eating and drinking but of righteousness and peace and joy in the Holy Spirit *(Romans 14:17 ESV)*.

As I remember your tears, I long to see you, that I may be filled with joy *(2 Timothy 1:4 ESV)*.

PEACE

Peace is usually described as a time when there is no war or conflict. But it is also a feeling that you have when you are no longer anxious or disturbed about something. I'm sure that you've heard about different wars throughout history and how everyone celebrated the time of peace when it finally arrived. There are pictures of people dancing in the streets and having picnics when World War II ended. Peace had finally arrived. How relieved they felt now that the fighting had ceased.

EXTRA FACT: The 20th century was the most in violent in recorded history. Wars caused the deaths of about 187 million people.

> **Ask Yourself**
>
> • Does Matthew 24:6 help when you hear of war?
> • When do you hear the word peace most often?
> • How do you have peace in daily-life?

The Peace of God is like the peace at the end of a war – it's an event. The conflict is over. Before God brought you into his family you were his enemy. When God changes you so that you love him, you are now his friend. You are at peace with him. It's not just an event, however, it's also an experience.

Imagine you are feeling anxious – that might not be hard to do. You've got a whole pile of problems. There's nobody that you can ask for help. You're a stranger in a strange place. That feeling you are experiencing is the opposite to peace.

Now imagine that you're in a place where you feel comfortable and there are friends who love you – all of a sudden you know, ,*This is where I belong. Phew!*,

All the problems you had are not problems anymore when you can share them with people who care for you. That is a feeling of peace.

Christians experience peace when Christ is in their lives. When you are part of God's family, you are finally where you were always meant to be. You are safe – whatever happens.

LÓÒK UP

Matthew 6:25-34. How would it change your life if you did this?

There is a famous Christian writer called Augustine who said – our hearts are restless until we find rest in God. God is the only source of true peace for your world, for your family, for you. You will still sometimes feel anxious and worried, but God tells you not to worry or be anxious about anything. Give him all your problems and concerns. He knows what to do.

AND THERE'S MORE!

PATIENCE

Have you ever heard this little poem?

Patience is a virtue,
possess it if you can.
Seldom found in women,
never found in man. (Jonathan Morris)

Now before all the guys reading this start getting on my case – I don't believe that. But I do believe that it is difficult to be patient.

God is very patient with us. When you read the Bible you will see other words that are sometimes used instead of patience – words like *steadfast* or *slow to anger*. Your Bible might use the word *long-suffering*. All these words mean the same thing: that you can tolerate delay, problems, or suffering without becoming annoyed or anxious. God has an abundance of patience as he waits for his children to trust in him and obey him. But be warned, this patience doesn't last forever. God was patient at the time of Noah – but he eventually sent the flood. We often lose our tempers very quickly but God holds back his anger. His anger with sin is just. Yet he shows great patience by being slow to show this anger and being quick to show mercy. However, the Lord will not leave the guilty unpunished.

 **2 Peter 3:8-9; Nahum 1:3 and Psalm 86:15.**

What do these Bible verses tell you about God's patience?

God tells us to be patient. He tells us to be patient when things go wrong. Trust in God in the middle of those difficult times. You may be frustrated when you see things going well for people who do not follow God's ways – again God tells us to relax. He has things under control.

Rejoice in hope, be patient in tribulation *(Romans 12:12 ESV).*

Be still before the Lord and wait patiently for him; fret not yourself over the one who prospers in his way, over the man who carries out evil devices! *(Psalm 37:7 ESV).*

GOODNESS

The word good is a word you might use after a delicious pizza. 'Man, that was good!' If someone is helpful and kind they are described as a good person. Goodness is a collection of many good qualities and actions.

But when God asks us to be good he is asking you to be more than just useful – he is asking you not to choose evil. He is asking you to trust and obey him. God is good and he is the best good – his goodness goes further than anyone else's. He is full of good.

He demonstrates his goodness by giving good things. He is a loving Heavenly Father and delights to give his children good gifts. He gives us these even without our asking – sunshine, air, life. God gives them because he is good.

Sometimes there are other things that we ask for – help, comfort, a job, a family. God will sometimes give these good gifts. But the greatest gift that he can give us is salvation – being saved from sin through the death and resurrection of Jesus Christ.

BIBLE PROOF

No one is good except God alone *(Mark 10:18 ESV)*.

The Lord is good, a stronghold in the day of trouble; and He knows those who take refuge in him *(Nahum 1:7 ESV)*.

LOOK UP

Matthew 7:11. What does this verse teach you about God?

Psalm 107:8-9. What does God give to people who are hungry for him?

FAITHFULNESS

When someone is loyal it means that they can be relied on. You can count on a loyal friend to always be there to help out, or just sing loudly on your birthday. A loyal sports fan will be there supporting the team every time a match is on – whether it is home or away.

Faithfulness is another word for loyalty. Sometimes in the Bible you will read the word *steadfast* which means the same thing. The person who is faithful and steadfast towards God consistently obeys him and loves him.

When you're consistent in something it means that you always do it. If you're consistently following God then you are faithful. But if you are faithful to God you are only faithful because he was faithful in the first place.

BIBLE PROOF

He who calls you is faithful; he will surely do it *(1 Thessalonians 5:24 ESV).*

> God is faithful, by whom you were called into the fellowship of his Son, Jesus Christ our Lord *(1 Corinthians 1:9 ESV)*.

God is faithful because he always keeps his promises. Everything he says he will do, he does. Even if you do not obey him in the way that you should. Even if you don't do all the things that you promised God you would – he is still faithful. He still keeps his promises. He is always faithful because that is who he is – it would be impossible for him to be anything else.

BIBLE PROOF

> It is impossible for God to lie *(Hebrews 6:18 ESV)*.

> If we are faithless, he remains faithful for he cannot deny himself *(2 Timothy 2:13 ESV)*.

GENTLENESS

Sometimes words like gentleness, kindness and peace are very like each other. It's almost as if they are part of a family of words and hang out together in stories and sentences because they describe the same situations. If you are a gentle person it is likely you are also kind. When people are around you they will feel at peace. Some people might describe you as tender, a calming person to have in their life.

Don't make the mistake of thinking that a gentle person is a weak person with no strength. When you are gentle you don't choose violence, but it doesn't mean that you can't stand up for yourself and others. In fact, a gentle person can also be firm and strong minded. They can certainly be brave!

Jesus is one of the perfect examples of gentleness. He was gentle with children. Where others wanted to get rid of them for being a pesky nuisance, Jesus welcomed little children.

He was caring to people who suffered from disease. He was compassionate to people who were sad or hungry.

Often in the Bible we read about the gentle, caring Jesus. He healed lepers, fed crowds, comforted widows. But Jesus' perfect love and care means that he is both gentle and strong and willing to defeat enemies in whatever way is necessary. He showed strength when he threw over the money-lenders tables in the temple.

The money-lenders were not showing love and care for the worship of God. Jesus' heart is so passionate about worshipping God in the right way. He's no push-over. So that's why he pushed over those tables. The people selling from them were not there to pray but to steal from people who wanted to show their love to God. He spoke harsh words when he needed to and words of forgiveness even to people who had let him down. That is Jesus – strong and gentle, gentle and strong!

When he was arrested by the authorities he could have used violent words but didn't. He could have fought back but chose to be gentle. He accepted death so that through his death sinners could be freed from the punishment of sin.

LOOK UP

John 2:13-17; Matthew 27:11-14; Matthew 4:23; Matthew 14:21 and Luke 7:11-15. What do these Bible verses show you about Jesus' care and his power?

Ask Yourself

- Who is the most patient person you've met?

- What is something you are always slow to do?

- What is something that you will always do quickly?

- How do you know something is good?

- What is lovely about loyalty?

- What actions show gentleness and strength? Are there jobs where you have to have both?

YOU YOURSELF!

SELF-CONTROL

What kind of things do you need to control in your life? You might have to control a family pet, particularly if it's a dog that likes to run off. You will control it by taking it for a walk on a leash. Sometimes you need to get your garden under control if it has become overgrown. Controlling something means to influence or direct something.

Toddlers need simple directions to keep them safe. If they are playing in the garden their parents will check that the gate is closed so that the child is controlled and not allowed to wander freely into dangerous traffic. Self-control is like that but instead of being controlled by someone else we make the decisions and take the actions to control ourselves.

Why do we need to do that? It's not like we're a bouncy dog that is a bit crazy and running all over the place. It's not like we're a very young kid who doesn't know about road safety. Why do we need to be controlled?

Our sinful desires are what need to be controlled. Often the things that we want to do are not good for us to do. Our emotions can become heated. Our desires to do things that are against God's law take over us and so our sins of thoughts become sins of actions.

The Apostle Paul understood this: 'For I do not do the good I want, but the evil I do not want is what I keep on doing' (Romans 7:19). Sometimes even good things can become bad things in our lives when they become more important to us than they should be.

Can you picture a beautiful chocolate birthday cake? It's lovely to enjoy a slice of cake at a celebration. But it might be that our selfish desires would make us take two, three or four slices – and then we'd be sick.

There are other things that God has created for us which are meant to be good for us. Men and women have been created to love each other and God has even given them the special relationship of marriage as a beautiful way to show that love to each other. But when men and women don't follow God's law they choose to love in wrong ways by behaving like a husband and wife without being married. Sometimes they decide to love other people instead of the people they are married to.

Showing self-control with your emotions means that you do not behave like a married person when you are not actually married.

When you don't practice self-control as a young person you will probably not do it when you are older – and then things get really messy. If you don't practice self-control with your pocket money, then you won't practice self control with your wages. When you are older other people will depend on you for food and clothing so it's important to be wise about what you spend your money on.

If you don't practice self-control with loving someone of the opposite sex when you are unmarried, then you will probably not do it when you are married. And when you are married you may have children and children need mothers and fathers to be wise and kind and loving. When couples are not faithful to each other, it breaks a lot of hearts.

The Bible has an interesting picture-story which describes someone without self-control. In Bible times if you lived in a city the main part of that city would be surrounded by large walls. Sometimes farmers and other people lived outside the walls, but if an enemy army approached, all the people from the surrounding area would seek refuge within the walls of the city. Soldiers would stand on the top of the walls and fire weapons on the enemy. Sometimes a city with impressive protective walls could keep an army at bay for weeks. But in Proverbs 25:28 it describes someone without self-control as being like a city that has been broken into and the walls destroyed. There is nothing left to protect it anymore.

Many wrong decisions lead to terrible consequences. An overpowering desire to have pleasure for ourselves can lead to pain and sorrow.

Perhaps you think, 'All I have to do is follow the rules and I'll be fine.' But true self-control is more than that. It means that you need to give your heart and desires to Jesus – give him all areas of your life to rule over. Even your affections. When you love Christ with your whole heart you will be satisfied in a way you never have been before.

BIBLE PROOF

Love the LORD your God with all your heart and with all your soul and with all your strength (*Deuteronomy 6:5 NIV*).

Love the LORD your God with all your heart and with all your soul and with all your mind (*Matthew 22:37 NIV*).

Take delight in the LORD and he will give you the desires of your heart (*Psalm 37:4 NIV*).

In your presence THERE is fullness of joy (*Psalm 16:11 ESV*).

How did Jesus show self-control? There were many times where he could have made things easier for himself but didn't. He chose to become human, that wasn't easy. He left heaven to come to earth. And he submitted to God's plan of death. This was a time when he really wanted something else, but he chose to submit himself to God the Father. Jesus knew before it happened that he would have to die to save people from sin, he knew what was ahead of him and felt afraid, as any human being would. He prayed to God his father, 'My Father, if it be possible, let this cup pass from me; nevertheless, not as I will, but as you will' (Matthew 26:39). Jesus was willing to submit himself to God's desire. Jesus did not let his own desires take control.

When you come to know God and submit yourself to him as his follower or disciple, even in hard times you still know God and rejoice in him.

LOOK UP

Habakkuk 3:17-19. What do these verses tell us about God and times of trouble?

One day those who know God will have the exact opposite experience to suffering because victory will come. In fact , the Bible says they will be more than conquerors.

Think about the joy that is felt when someone wins a match or a race. Perhaps you can picture the relief someone feels when they complete an obstacle course or a marathon? What has been the hardest thing you have had to do? How did you feel when you completed the task? Now multiply that feeling by a hundred or more. God's people will be more than conquerors. In fact, because Jesus has done everything that is required for a complete victory we are already on the winning side. The war is won even though we still have to battle against our own sin. Jesus is the victor. He has won this victory not us. But we are still the conquerors - more than conquerors! We're on Team God!

BIBLE PROOF Who shall separate us from the love of Christ? Shall tribulation, or distress, or persecution, or famine, or nakedness, or danger, or sword? As it is written, "For your sake we are being killed all the day long; we are regarded as sheep to be slaughtered." No, in all these things we are more than conquerors through him who loved us. For I am sure that neither death nor life, nor angels nor rulers, nor things present nor things to come, nor powers, nor height nor depth, nor anything else in all creation; will be able to separate us from the love of God in. Christ Jesus our Lord *(Romans 8:35-39 ESV)*

- Why does Galatians 5:22-29 use the word fruit and not fruits?

Ask Yourself

- What happens when your team wins if you are a player?

- Why is it important that God rules your mind?

- Where do you feel the most safe? A life without self-control is like a life without safety.

- What did Jesus give up when he submitted to God the Father's plan for salvation? Picture what heaven must have been like for him.

WRAPPING UP

The Word of God is full of rich treasures about the truth of God and it is up to you to dig for this treasure yourself.

If you were presented with a large treasure chest full of gold and diamonds you would be excited. But you would be even more excited if you had found a treasure map and had taken a shovel to dig up the chest for yourself. When you work hard for something it means you appreciate it more. When you discover something for yourself you realise its true value.

It's the same with God and his Word.

The Bible is an important book full of truths about God. But it is also a book that has been written for you. It's as important as a library and as personal as a letter. And the author, God, has written it so that you can come to know him.

He says to you, 'Come to me, all who labour and are heavy laden, and I will give you rest' (Matthew 11:28).

Dig in God's Word and every time you come across a truth about him look at it and think about it. Pray to God. Ask him to show you what this truth really means.

If you really know God you will want to give everything to him, your time, your energy, your love. You will long to spend time with him in prayer. It will be as natural to you as snacks and breakfast. Your thoughts will focus on God in pretty much any situation you find yourself in. You will show courage by sharing with others the good news of salvation, because God will give you his strength. Knowing God like this gives you peace and contentment.

So get digging. Open God's Word for yourself. And make this a treasure hunt you enjoy for the rest of your life.

BIBLE PROOF For everything that was written in the past was written to teach us, so that through endurance and the encouragement of the Scriptures we might have hope *(Romans 15:4 NIV)*.

This is a prayer that Paul had for the church in Ephesus and that I also have for you:

I keep asking that the God of our Lord Jesus Christ, the glorious Father, may give you the Spirit of wisdom and revelation, so that you may know him better. I pray that the eyes of your heart may be enlightened in order that you may know the hope to which he has called you, the riches of his glorious inheritance in his holy people, and his incomparably great power for us who believe. That power is the same as the mighty strength he exerted when he raised Christ from the dead and seated him at his right hand in the heavenly realms, far above all rule and authority, power and dominion, and every name that is invoked, not only in the present age but also in the one to come. And God placed all things under his feet and appointed him to be head over everything for the church, which is his body, the fullness of him who fills everything in every way *(Ephesians 1: 17-23 NIV)*.

BiBLioGRAPHY

WEBSITES AND PODCASTS

Get a grip: The neuroscience of how we pick things up, The Boston Globe
https://www.bostonglobe.com/ideas/2015/08/27/
get-grip-the-neuroscience-how-pick-
things/3XPqgZMVEgMPmlYX0cMooK/story.html

Number of families in the UK
https://www.statista.com/statistics/281608/
number-of-families-in-the-uk/

Number of families in the US
https://www.statista.com/topics/1484/families/

Births in the US Statistics and Facts
https://www.statista.com/topics/4452/births-in-
the-us/#topicOverview

Number of Live births in the United Kingdom
https://www.statista.com/statistics/281981/live-
births-in-the-united-kingdom-uk/

The Ten Strongest Animals on Earth
a-z-animals.com

Top 10 Amazing Facts of the World
www.javapoint.com

The Simplicity of God by Sinclair Ferguson
https://www.ligonier.org/podcasts/things-unseen-
with-sinclair-ferguson/the-simplicity-of-god

The Fruit of the Spirit by R.C. Sproul
https://www.monergism.com/fruit-spirit-r-c-sproul#:~:text=It%20was%20ratified,a%20judgmental%20spirit.

What is Love by John Piper
https://www.desiringgod.org/interviews/what-is-love

BOOKS

AW Tozer *Three Spiritual Classics In One Volume: The Knowledge of the Holy, the Pursuit of God, and God's Pursuit of Man Moody Publishers, USA, Combined edition, 2018,* ISBN 978-1940177601

JI Packer, *Knowing God, Hodder and Stoughton,* United Kingdom, 3rd Edition, 2005, ISBN 978-0340863541

Sinclair B. Ferguson, *How Jesus Cares, Christian Focus Publications,* United Kingdom, 2022, ISBN 9781527108592

John Davis, *Seeing the Unseen God, Christian Focus Publications,* United Kingdom, 2023, ISBN 9781527110014

The Illustrated Westminster Shorter Catechism, Christian Focus Publications, United Kingdom, 2022, ISBN 9781527109025

AUTHOR PAGE

Catherine Mackenzie has written several biographies for young teens in the Trailblazer series as well as for younger children in the Little Lights series. She lives in Scotland in the United Kingdom and has several nieces and nephews.

Photography and scrap books are two of her hobbies.

She doesn't have any pets but likes to borrow other people's.

ISBN: 978-1-78191-521-9

ISBN: 978-1-85792-348-3

ISBN: 978-1-78191-057-3

ISBN: 978-1-78191-550-9

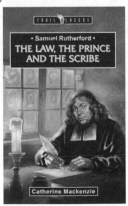

ISBN: 978-1-5271-0309-2

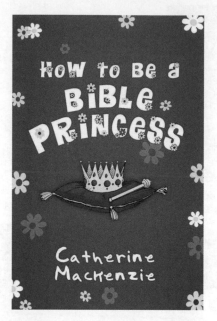

How to be a Bible Princess

ISBN: 978-1-84550-825-8

If you were a princess you'd have the best wardrobe in the world with new dresses in it every day - and a tiara to match. But is that all there is to being a princess? And what does it mean to be a real Bible princess? Abigail, Jehosheba, Esther and The Queen of the South were women and royalty who honoured God. Pharaoh's daughter and Michal were princesses who showed bravery but were they true followers of the Lord? Jezebel and Herodias' daughter are two royal women who did not love God. All their stories are in the Bible and all can teach us in their own way how to be a Bible princess, daughters of the King, women and girls of righteousness.

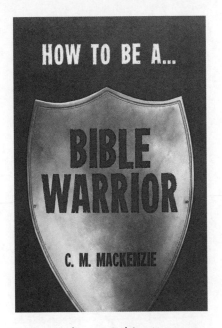

How to be a Bible Warrior

ISBN: 978-1-78191-231-7

If you were a warrior you'd have a sharp, shiny sword and an army of soldiers to fight with. But is that all there is to being a warrior? And what does it mean to be a Bible Warrior? Abraham, David, Moses, Joshua, Gideon and Jehoshaphat are all men from the Bible who fought in real life battles, but the lessons we learn from their lives are not about sword skills or battle tactics, they are about honouring God and glorifying him.

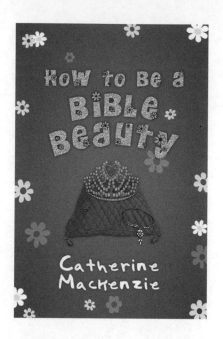

How to be a Bible Beauty

ISBN: 978-1-78191-578-3

Some people want to look beautiful, wearing the best clothes, with gorgeous hair, and pretty jewellery. But is that what beauty is all about? Anna was devoted to God and longed to meet the promised Messiah. Leah realised that skin beauty was not as important as trusting in God for your salvation and Dorcas showed her true beauty by showing God's love to others. All these stories and others like them are in the Bible. These Bible beauties can teach us how to be women of God, people with an eternal beauty that is more than skin deep!

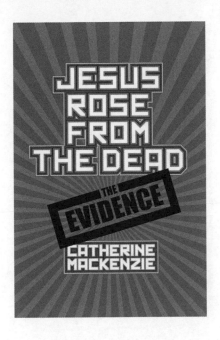

Jesus Rose from the Dead: The Evidence

ISBN: 978-1-84550-537-0

If you were to go out into the street with a questionnaire to find out what people thought about truth you would get a variety of answers. Some people think that the truth doesn't really matter. Sadly many people today instead of believing the truth about Jesus Christ, actually believe the lies that are told about him.

So what do you believe about Jesus Christ? Do you believe he rose from the dead? This book will help you find out the truth – and how this truth is not only amazing - it also makes sense!

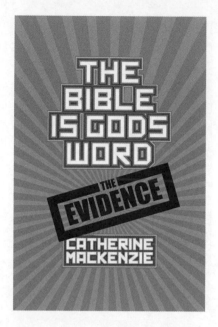

The Bible is God's Word: The Evidence

ISBN: 978-1-78191-555-4

What is the Bible anyway? Who wrote it? Is it really accurate and how can we know for sure that it is true – totally true?

These and other questions about the Word of God are answered in this book.

You don't have to be a professor to ask or answer these important questions but you can read the most amazing book ever written and you can trust it - because it is God's Word – the Bible.

You Might Also Like....

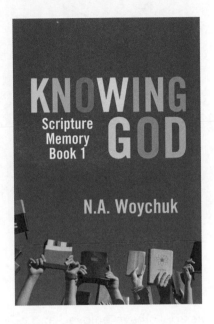

Knowing God: Scripture Memory Book

ISBN: 978-1-84550-779-4

There is one person you need to know — he is the most important person that you will ever know. God.

In this book there are eighty-four verses that you will learn and these are arranged into twelve assignments for you to work through. As you memorize these passages you will be studying the great truths about God himself.

God's Promises Kept

ISBN: 978-1-5271-0618-5

For many years adults have enjoyed and been blessed by the profound thinking and clear writing of Charles Haddon Spurgeon. Now this small padded book allows children to discover this joy for themselves. Following the premise of The Chequebook of the Bank of Faith, prolific children's author and editor Catherine Mackenzie has adapted Spurgeon's devotionals to be accessible to today's 9–14 year olds, allowing a new generation to treasure God's promises.

Each entry finishes with a suggestion for what the reader should do in response to what they have read, and a prayer.

More of God's Promises Kept

ISBN: 978-1-5271-0619-2

Following on from God's Promises Kept, Catherine Mackenzie gives us more devotions inspired by Charles Haddon Spurgeon's Chequebook of the Bank of Faith. By adapting Spurgeon's daily devotions to be accessible for today's 9–14 year olds, Catherine Mackenzie encourages a new generation to cling to the promises of God. This small padded book is a treasure trove that would be an idea gift for any child.

Each entry finishes with a suggestion for what the reader should do in response to what they have read, and a prayer.